John A. Wright

How to get Good Judges

A Study of the Defects of the Judicial Systems of the States

John A. Wright

How to get Good Judges
A Study of the Defects of the Judicial Systems of the States

ISBN/EAN: 9783337187996

Printed in Europe, USA, Canada, Australia, Japan

Cover: Foto ©Suzi / pixelio.de

More available books at **www.hansebooks.com**

FOR GENERAL READERS

How to Get Good Judges

A STUDY OF THE DEFECTS OF

THE JUDICIAL SYSTEMS OF THE STATES

WITH

A PLAN FOR A SCIENTIFIC JUDICIAL SYSTEM

BY

JOHN A. WRIGHT

Member of the Committee of the San Francisco Bar Association on the Judiciary

SAN FRANCISCO:

The S. Carson Company, Publishers

1892.

*" The object of the profession of the law, of jurisprudence
seen on its* PRACTICAL *side, is not so much that the law be
discovered and made known, as that it be applied and
obeyed."*

PROFESSOR LORIMER.

HOW TO GET GOOD JUDGES.

I.

POPULAR DISTRUST OF THE JUDICIARY — ITS NATURE AND CAUSES.

No honest and sensible man who reads the newspapers and converses with his fellows can deny that a large class of people throughout the United States entertains a growing distrust of our judges and judicial systems. This distrust prevails, undoubtedly, to a greater extent in some States than in others, and among some classes more than among others. It exists side by side with the utmost respect for the character and attainments of particular courts and particular judges. Sometimes it appears in some old State, and is attributed to special and passing conditions; sometimes it appears in

some new State, and is said to be the natural
result of crude conditions and heterogeneous
society. At an early period in California, the
scorn of the judiciary and judicial methods, as
means to beneficial ends, was so great among
the best classes in the community that the Vigilance Committee arose to do lawless justice ;
many years later, in Louisiana, a similar mental attitude on the part of the people provoked a
disgraceful, though perhaps unavoidable, massacre. In almost every State of the West and
South, during the long time between the period of the California Vigilance Committee and
that of the New Orleans Committee, there have
been lynchings innumerable, because neither
the judicial system nor the judges were trusted.
For full forty years the same political disease
has in some form appeared in almost every
State in the Union, and we are apparently no
nearer its cure to-day than when it first horri-
fied Americans. Recently, in New York, certain judges were forced by operation of law to
confess that they had bought their nomina-
tions. Some form of distrust surely arises
against them. Are we to go on forever so far
distrusting our judges and judicial systems that

we must on occasion seek relief in murder, massacre, and riot?

Some recent manifestations of the distrustful attitude of the public mind towards the judiciary in the State of California have prompted the publication of this essay. For so long as feeling has not taken the form of violence, there seems some hope that the suggestions here offered will be patiently and attentively examined with a view toward their adoption, if apparently practicable. Indeed I have noticed, (or thought I had), evidence that the remedies which I shall propose were at last dimly discerned by some honest and thoughtful minds in Louisiana, and this gives me further hope that they will be somewhere weighed with care. Moreover, the marvelous strides which scientific methods to reform the ballot and the civil service have made in the minds of all classes, still further encourage me to offer a proposal for the reformation of the most important branch of our State governments by means which will be found to be in their nature born of the political ideas and aspirations that gave birth to the Australian ballot system, the modern notions of a proper civil service, and the American system of free public schools.

For the benefit of such readers as may not be familiar with the recent events in the State of California, as well as for the purpose of pointing to the primary grounds for public distrust of the judges, I shall open with a brief statement of recent occurrences in California, confining myself, however, exclusively to the manifestations of distrust contained in those occurrences. The grounds of distrust are fundamentally the same everywhere as in California, but California at this time happens to offer especially clear evidence of the sources of disease. With slight variations the remedies must be the same if the disease is the same.

A great public question recently arose out of the action of one of the judges of our Superior Court in undertaking to impanel a Grand Jury for the city of San Francisco by means of an elisor, without the intervention of the Sheriff. Rumors had filled the air that the State Legislature and the Municipal Boards were corrupt, root and branch—were, indeed, but organized bands of public plunderers existing for years under the leadership of political bosses of the most degraded and skillful type. The judge referred to assembled and swore in a body of

citizens as a Grand Jury, who immediately issued subpœnas summoning several persons as
witnesses, who were said to have some knowledge of corruption in public place.   One of
these witnesses refused to obey the subpœna
on the ground that the Grand Jury was not
regularly organized.   He was brought up for
contempt before the judge who formed the jury,
and convicted.   But immediately another judge
of the same Court issued a writ of *habeas cor-
pus*, reviewed the commitment, declared the
Grand Jury unlawful, and released the prisoner.   Then there was assembled a public meeting which denounced in unmeasured terms the
judge who released the prisoner, ascribing to
him base subservience to the mandates of a
faction said to be interested in thwarting the
inquiry of the Grand Jury, with this reason for
the subservience added: *That he owed his nom-
ination and election to the faction.*   The spectacle
of one judge of a Court reversing the act of another judge of the same Court without possessing appellate jurisdiction, was forcibly com-
mented on.   Another witness, summoned by
the same Grand Jury, undertook to get the
opinion of the Supreme Court (the highest Ap-

pellate Court) on the legality of the Grand
Jury, in order to set the matter at rest. Ac-
cordingly, he refused to obey, was committed
for contempt, but sued out a writ of *habeas cor-
pus* from the Supreme Court, and not from another judge of the lower Court. The Supreme
Court held the summons lawful and the commitment authorized. The public press then
teemed with explanations and illustrations of
the rebuke, presumed to be implied in this
action of the Supreme Court, to the judge who
released the first recalcitrant witness. The
Grand Jury proceeded with its work, and in
due time found an indictment against a member of the late Legislature for corruption in
office. The indicted legislator immediately applied to the Supreme Court for a writ of pro-
hibition, to prevent any trial from taking place
in the Court below, on the ground that the
Grand Jury had been unlawfully summoned,
and therefore could not indict him. His application was argued in the Supreme Court
most elaborately by counsel on both sides, and
submitted for decision. While it was under
consideration, the newspaper press cajoled and
threatened the Court in a manner that I am

certain was never before witnessed in a civil-
ized community. Undoubtedly, all the "corrupt influences" of the State were opposed to
the existence of the Grand Jury, but in support of the cause of "honesty," the newspapers
who espoused that side did not hesitate to
threaten the judges with the election of a Legislature that would summarily remove them
from office if they decided in favor of the point
raised by the prisoner. The same newspapers
insinuated that some of the judges were offered
(by interests opposed to the Grand Jury and
its work) appointments on the vacant Federal
Bench, and warned the judges not to swallow
the bait. The whole tone of the newspaper
press expressed the idea that the several judges
of the Supreme Court were creatures of political faction, hoping for promotion only through
subserviency to the powers that created them.
A majority of the Court sustained the law
point made on behalf of the prisoner; the
Grand Jury was declared unlawful, and he was
discharged. Then, again, the press attacked
the Court more fiercely and bitterly than ever,
and again the key-note of the attack was a reference to the methods and men, by means of

which the several judges were nominated. Finally, the judge of the lower Court, whose action had been reviewed and reversed, assembled the unlawful Grand Jury, and from the Bench pronounced to them a carefully prepared opinion, criticizing and controverting the reasoning of the Supreme Court. This action was pronounced heroic by one section of the press, and by another demagogic and subversive of all ideas of judicial decorum and good government.

It is not to the purpose to ask, what in reality are the characters of those men who in California have been so fiercely assailed? The vilest scandals have been circulated from time to time against so many other judges in California, both by public gossip and public print, without an effective demand from any source, either for punishment or vindication; the judges are changed so often, and old scandals are so readily forgotten by the public when new ones appear, that public opinion has become contemptible in the eyes of honest and dishonest judges alike. The very judge who impaneled and supported this Grand Jury, and who at the end of the litigation was on the

topmost wave of popular esteem, only a few
months before he impaneled the Grand Jury
was himself the object of a newspaper attack,
if possible more virulent and scandalous than
that made on the abused Court that disbanded
his Grand Jury. An honorable man who fully
appreciates the lofty nature of judicial functions will shrink from ascribing to any judge,
without the most convincing evidence, a design
to shape his decisions so as to win favor with
the people as utterly as he would shrink from
ascribing to any judge, a design to win the
favor of a clique: for " popularity " or " unpopularity," whether with a large class or with
a small class, is, if it influences a judge, as
much a bribe to him as money. It is far from
my purpose to make mean insinuations against,
or institute invidious comparisons between
any of the judges to whom I have alluded. I
ascribe no reasons for their decisions except
those given in their official opinions. I desire
to point out merely, that, from time to time,
all shades of opinion, respecting the conduct of
all the judges indifferently, were indulged in
with readiness, except the opinion that they
would of necessity be governed by their judi-

cial oaths, indifferent to public or private favor, and competent to arrive at correct conclusions. Many of them I know (and doubtless others of them whom I do not know) enjoy in their private circles the highest respect and admiration of a large number of honorable men and women ; and, humanly speaking, the insight into the character and motives of a man which is obtained by his personal acquaintances is the best knowledge we can obtain of him. I am not dealing with their private characters, but with the fact that from time to time the press and other influences have made it appear, and honest people have believed, whether justly or unjustly, that those judges have been governed in their official action either by the basest bias towards and subordination to the corrupt ends of great corporations, factions, and private interests, or by the equally base purpose of winning popularity or avoiding unpopularity with the masses.

Nor do I intend to argue, as many worthy (and all unworthy) lawyers argue, that the reputations of our courts and judges have suffered merely because the press is wantonly licentious or moved by vicious lust of money

and political power. The assertion is made
idly when it is not knowingly false. Were our
judicial system as vigorous and well adapted to
fulfil its functions as is our press, not alone
would the reputations of our courts and judges
be unassailable, but there could exist no licentious use of free speech. Any judicial system •
is demonstrated to be rotten, or at least in-
effectual, if we assert that a vicious press has
power to blast the reputations of the courts.
One of the very foremost purposes of a judicial system is to protect reputations—those of
its own officers included. If it be a healthy
judicial system, it will accomplish this purpose
by creating and fostering in its members wor-
thiness palpable to all men ; if it be an un-
healthy system, it will aim rather to ·suppress
criticism. The truth is, the rude vigor with
which the press asserts and exercises the function of criticizing the judicial system to the people, and the weakness with which the judicial
system sustains the attack before the people,
demonstrates in the highest degree the value
of free, and, on occasion, of *very* free speech.
The weak spot is pointed out, and though nau-
seous medicine is administered, with the bless-

ing of Providence, it may prove the means to
a cure.

We know that all these courts were constituted, and all these judges elected, by methods prescribed by the people, not carelessly
or indifferently, but with the most jealous
and scrupulous regard on the part of the people for their own interests. We know that
every effort has been made to keep the courts
and judges in "touch with the people," and to
prevent them from becoming tyrannous, auto-
cratic, aristocratic, ·bureaucratic, or anything
else ghost-like and horrible to the popular
imagination. Salaries are kept low that the
judges may not have proud stomachs ; term of
office is made short in order that they may un-
derstand that they are servants who must earn
the approval of their masters, and solicit re-
employment as a grace and a favor, not in any
degree as a right earned. Yet, notwithstanding all the devices and desires of the people,
notwithstanding they reserve strict control,
they have not succeeded in getting courts or
judges in whom they place that confidence
that a master should have in his chief employees.

And we know, or at least we may fairly assume, that some high-minded men on the Bench have suffered or may suffer obloquy for the faults of base men and a base system : for trial by newspaper or public gossip is not adapted to the purpose of reaching nicely accurate conclusions. And we know that suspicious and ungenerous masters have no right to find trusty and faithful servants. Can judges who may be one day on the summit of "popularity" and another day in the depths of "unpopularity" administer real, impartial, God-given justice between man and man for any long space? Must they not sometimes be tempted to suit their decisions so as to win favor and obtain promotion from the people—or from some one else ? If many of them yield to such temptation, or if even we suspect them to yield, are they to us any longer judges ? Are they not rather mere political hirelings ? And should we not better at once discard the pretense that we have any judicial system whatever ?

Do we not present a pitiful, nay, contemptible, aspect to humanity ? This government is part of ourselves. And if we are afflicted

with a loathsome disease, should we make an
exhibition to the world of our sores? If we
proclaim to humanity that we are incompetent
to create efficient tribunals, or to select just
judges, how can we hope to be respected?
How can we expect our children to grow up
with love of country, or regard for morality?
If a government can secure to us neither prop-
erty nor honor, how long shall we endure it?
And though *we* may be willing to live our lives
in cowardly suspicion and distrust of those to
whom we commit the sacred trust of adminis-
tering justice, shall not a better generation
arise to destroy a system of government that
debases the soul of man?

Let us look the facts plainly in the face.

We cannot go on forever distrusting our
judges. If the day is not approaching when
we shall put faith in the impartiality of our
tribunals, the day is approaching when an end
will be put to our present form of civil society.
I dare not think that Republican institutions
on the American continent are doomed to die
of corruption. But I do think it is high time
that something was done to restore confidence
in our institutions, and I am certain that until

we shall establish a judicial system possessing the utmost confidence and respect of the people, we cannot make a sure step toward any other substantial improvement in government.

That absolute confidence in the ability and integrity of the law officers of the State would go far toward preventing corruption and mal-administration in all branches of the government—nay, would almost entirely reform the government—is a proposition which will commend itself to any one who comprehends the mighty influence which the law officers of the State have upon the government. The object of this essay is to suggest means of creating and *justifying* confidence in the law officers of the government.

And I think it must be apparent that *at the bottom of our distrust in our Courts and judges lie the facts that under our present system the great corporations and private interests of the State, the corrupt politicians, their retainers and patrons, are the persons by whom our judges are principally nominated and elected, and that we have no adequate means of disciplining or vindicating our judges when their reputations are assailed.*

So long as any method of selecting the judges is employed that is palpably amenable to political influences of a low order, so long shall we necessarily feel this distrust. For this reason a system of selecting the judges by appointment of the Governor, with or without the consent of the Legislature, would only be a shade better than the present system. Governors, as well as political conventions, may be influenced in their choice by unworthy motives and are no more competent to select the best men. Therefore, some system of selection radically different from any yet tried; some system adapted in a more scientific manner than any that has hitherto been suggested to the task of obtaining the best men for the place, must be found and put in practice before we shall feel that perfect trust in the impartiality of our judges so essential to our self-respect and prosperity as an organized community.

But there is another ground for the diminished public respect for our high tribunals. During the past forty years the law Courts throughout the United States have steadily become less capable of satisfactorily dispatching

business. Never at any period in the history
of the race has justice been more unconscion-
ably delayed. Yet, during these forty years
of decadence in businesslike efficiency on the
part of our Courts, a steady and marvelous
growth of that very ability which the Courts
lack has created and fostered gigantic corporations, private fortunes and enormous enter-
prises of all kinds. There is no comparison
between the efficiency for its ends of the greatest Court of many a great State, and the efficiency for its ends of a Board of Directors of
many a corporation under the ostensible jurisdiction of the State. Until the Courts are on a
par with private organizations in capacity for
work ; until litigation is promptly and efficient-
ly dispatched, public respect for our tribunals
will not be what it should be.

The causes of this business inefficiency of
our judicial system are not many nor far to
seek. The chief cause is, that during these
forty years, the talent and industry that should
have been engaged on the bench and in the
administrative law offices, in developing the
science of jurisprudence for the benefit of the
whole people, have been attracted by greater

rewards to the support of the private interests
I have alluded to ; have been repelled from the
public service by State parsimony and public
distrust.

Of course, there are exceptions to this gener-
alization. Sometimes a State offers its judges
compensation and security of tenure of office
somewhat approaching in value the rewards of
private practice; then admiration for the functions of judicial office—which, thank heaven,
is still ingrained in lawyers — attracts occasionally a thoroughly able man to the service
of the State. But the number of such men
(in most of the States) is insufficient to accomplish any great result, and is inconsiderable
compared to the number of able men remain-
ing at the bar in the service of great private
interests. Now, in order to accomplish anything in the way of substantial law reform, the
Bench and the administrative law officers of
the State, as a class, should be markedly
superior in experience and capacity to the
remainder of the bar as a class. It must be
evident that so long as better work is done in
waging litigation at the bar than is done by
the Bench in terminating litigation, the mass

of law suits will grow. While judges are generally inferior in capacity to the lawyers employed by private interests, public interests are necessarily delayed and thwarted. No reform in mere procedure can prevent it.

That at present the general effectiveness of the lawyers who serve great private interests is markedly greater than the general effectiveness of the lawyers in the public service, cannot be questioned. Shall we wonder, then, that the efforts of the former class must—slowly, intermittently, imperceptibly, perhaps, but still steadily—prevail in all minor conflicts between public policy and private interests ?

Let us ask ourselves a courageous question : If this tendency to general combination between persons of great wealth, persons of great business capacity and persons of great legal attainments be not arrested or counterbalanced what shall come to the " plain people of the United States " ? Class government or —— ?

" The monopolies have the best lawyers; the State can only now and then get other than second-rate men." Such is and has been for a long time the universal observation. But

are not the causes obvious? " The monopolies " offer the greatest careers that professional
attainments can reach in the life of an American lawyer to-day; and *ability alone* is the passport to these careers. The monopolies ask for
the utmost loyalty and the best efforts of the
men who serve them, but they offer in ex-
change wealth, social consideration, relief from
anxiety; thus they keep the minds of those
they employ free for and encouraged to the
utmost exertion. But the State offers no
career at all comparable to this; its service
attracts few men of eminent ability, seriously
sensible of the responsibilities they owe to
themselves and their families. Nor is capacity
alone the passport to the State's service, but
the favor of politicians. Offices that call for
the noblest qualities of the human mind must
be sought through the paths of low political
intrigue ; and the reward offered to a lofty
mind for this abasement is a stinted compensation, an insecure tenure—no provision for
growing domestic necessities, no provision for
old age, not even public confidence. How can
we expect dispatch of business and independence of conduct on the part of our judges if

the only stimulus we offer them consists of
such nice problems as how to make ends meet
at home, how to secure a re-nomination and
how to account for the " luck" of men who
" amass fortunes at the bar in doing work of
the same character " (if not the same quality)
" for which men on the bench are rewarded
with anxiety and humiliation " ?

II.

GENERAL NATURE OF THE REMEDIES.

The general nature of the remedies to be applied to this state of things is sufficiently obvious, but the means of applying the remedies could only be discovered by diligent thought and observation. I believe, however, that those means are now within our reach, though I fear we may not have the courage to adopt them. I do not mean to say we can weed the bench, the law offices of the State, and the bar, at once, and by a single act, of all incompetent and unworthy persons. The weeds, through a long course of stupid neglect, have been allowed to grow to surpassing luxuriance ; but I do confidently submit that a system can be devised on lines that will, *in time*, accomplish the results we have in view, so far as those results are attainable outside of Paradise.

In general terms we must aim :

1st. To make a career in the service of the State more attractive to lawyers than any career at the bar ;

2nd. To make entrance to the legal service of the State, as far as possible, unattainable by any but the most suitable men at the bar ;

3rd. To make dismissal from the service of the State certain to follow misconduct ; and,

4th. To elevate the character and capacity of the entire bar.

These ends cannot be reached in a day, nor yet in a year under any system. Under the present system they never can be reached. And I do not lose sight of the fact that whatever system be devised it must work with and upon the material we now have at the bar and on the Bench, good, bad or indifferent as that material may be.

Common sense points out that (except, perhaps, in the City of New York, where the judges receive salaries of $17,500 a year) the first thing to be done toward reaching our end is to exercise more liberality ; to increase largely the salaries of the judges ; to increase considerably the salaries of all other law officers, and to make tenure of office dependent

on good behavior. Able lawyers will then
turn their attention to the public service.

If the people want the best lawyers in their
service — and we know that the want is
urgent—then the people must outbid the " mo-
nopolists " in competition for such men. The
people are the greatest and the richest corporation within the limits of the State. Why
should they hesitate ? How long can they be
powerful if their rivals or enemies possess the
services of the ablest men in the community ?
What would any one say of the good sense of a
commercial or manufacturing house possessed
of practically unlimited capital, and engaged
in a most important, extensive and compli-
cated business, that nevertheless refused to
pay its most indispensable employees what
they are offered by rival houses of small importance ?

Lest I should be misunderstood in respect
to the extent of the emoluments that a State
should offer, I assert that on moral grounds
quite apart from any grounds of expediency
the salary of a Justice of the Highest Appellate
Court should not be less than the salary of the
highest paid official in any private corporation

in the State, and the respective salaries of the
Judges of the Superior Courts should be pro-
portionately dignified.   There is no Court in
the State, above that of Justice of the Peace,
that does not administer affairs, merely financial, of quite as much importance as the affairs
of many corporations, and, that does not require of its presiding magistrate, for the proper discharge of his duty, higher mental and
moral qualities than any private business,
however extensive.   Consider the enormous
financial interests finally disposed of by the
Supreme Appellate Courts every year and the
enormous fortunes that pass through the Pro-
bate Courts.   But, apart from the merely
financial importance of the work done by our
Courts, no bank or railroad corporation affects
the rights, morals and growth of the whole
people of the State to half the extent that one
Court does.   To obtain the best men for our
Courts is a moral duty ; it is no less a moral
duty to offer them commensurate reward.   If
it is worth while for the stockholders of Wells,
Fargo & Co. and the California Bank to offer
their respective presidents salaries of $15,000
or $20,000 a year, how much is worth the while

of the people of the great State of California
to offer their Chief Justice ?

Even if the scale of salaries which I suggest
be adopted, the best judicial salary would not
be at all equal to the income of some of the
leading lawyers to-day at the bar. But if tenure of office were made " during good behavior," with a provision for retirement at a certain age like that granted by the Federal Government, the service of the State would be
attractive to almost every lawyer who leads
at the bar, though to enter it might involve
some financial sacrifice. Really high attainments in the profession of the law are rarely
accompanied by absolute sordidness. A broad
philosophical study of the law, successfully
applied to the affairs of every day life (even
under the lowering influences that now sur-
round the profession) breeds — nay, requires,
generosity and honesty of spirit. If avarice
and its accompanying vices are bred by the
modern practice of the law in some men who
would not otherwise fall, it is because the
people by their fatal policy of penuriousness
and absurd dread of " founding an aristo-
cracy " allow profit and honor to be dispensed

solely by avaricious clients. And yet, financial ease, reasonable provisions for a growing family, and reasonable security against old age and sickness, may be offered by the State without offering great fortunes. And honor may, likewise, be offered by the State without breeding the slightest aristocratic tendency, if the State will make the road to its service such an one as high minded and competent men may pursue.

Having made the office of judge attractive, it becomes at once an object of desire as well to the unworthy as to the worthy ; consequently, without a system adequate to prevent the office from being captured by political methods, there would be little advantage in making it desirable to worthy men. It is plain that merely to stimulate the desire of all classes of men at the bar to be judges or law officers of the State would not make it certain that the best and most suitable persons among those who entertained the desire would succeed in obtaining the coveted place. And while it is essential for the proper administration of law that every lawyer should, from the moment of entering

into his profession, look forward to a place
upon the Bench as the highest reward which
his professional life could reach, it would be
a lamentable error if that ambition, so worthy
in itself, could only be gratified by means of
chicanery and intrigue. Not alone must desire to serve the State be stimulated in the
best men, but the entire career of a lawyer
should, so far as possible, be a continued training for the worthy and efficient discharge of
judicial functions. The bar should be so organized that unworthiness would be equivalent
to failure, would be almost invariably a preventive to the highest success, while real merit
would plainly appear to be the only road to
fortune. "It is important, above all other
things, to properly define and stimulate the
moral character of the advocate—the advocate
considered in the spontaneity and intimacy of
his actions, independently of his dealings with
other people." The most essential qualities in
a judge are precisely the most essential and
rare qualities in an advocate. Probity, disinterestedness, moderation and independence are
as essential to a great lawyer as to a great
judge. From plain virtues alone should power

come. Some ancient writer speaking on this subject has said, " one cannot be a perfect advocate if one be not a good and honest man."

So it becomes an essential part of any system that shall attempt to give us any approach to a perfect judiciary, not only that the system should offer adequate reward for worth and promote the growth of those qualities in members of the bar that produce good, great judges, but should be adequate to exclude unworthy persons from the judiciary — put it beyond their reach.

The problem of how to make entrance to the legal service of the State unattainable by any but the most suitable men at the bar necessarily involves the problem of how to elevate the character and capacity of the entire bar. But it is plain that to accomplish any marked elevation of the character and capacity of an entire class requires time and care, while in the meantime we must have judges and should have the best that the present material at our command affords. I have, therefore, aimed to provide a system which shall contain temporary expedients tending to set in operation and promote the growth of the general scheme.

Adequate reward is the first essential, as I have pointed out. But measurably to prevent the offices in the judicial service of the State from falling to inefficient and untried men, as so often happens under the present system, I propose next to render every man ineligible to the Bench, until he shall have continuously practiced for at least ten years at the bar. I shall not stay to argue the question whether any man, whatever his talents, can be mature enough to administer properly the affairs of a court of record, without at least ten years' experience at the bar. I content myself with pointing out, what no man can deny, that ten years' experience at the bar will at least be some training that may with advantage be undergone by the greatest "natural genius." But, above all, this requirement will be some immediate barrier against the capture of such offices by certain so-called lawyers who are really mere politicians; it will limit the choice of judicial candidates to persons whose characters have become somewhat well known; thus, though it is intended to form part of the general system which I propose, the immediate advantage of such provision, even under the present conditions of the bar, must be apparent.

This brings me to the heart of the system which I have in mind. How can we select from among those men at the bar, who have been ten years in practice, those best qualified to be our judges ? Can we devise some scheme by which, making allowance for human error, we shall get the best attainable men ?

An examination of the faults inherent in the methods hitherto employed by us has led me to believe that such a scheme can be devised. The scheme which commends itself to me I shall endeavor to unfold as it developed itself in my mind.

I shall first speak of the fault inherent in the method originally employed in the United States, viz.: appointment by the Executive. This method has apparently now produced in England judges whose probity is unquestioned by any class of the English people; but apparently the same method at one time produced utterly unworthy judges in England, while in the United States, after long trial, it was rejected by the people of most of the States. I think the people of the United States were right in rejecting the method of appointing judges empolyed in the early history of the republic. Governors and executive officers did not use the power entrusted to them wisely or well. But the early American method of appointment, and the early English method from which it was borrowed, were not in reality the same as the modern English method.

The difference is this : While the early American governor and the English Crown had absolute power to select any member of the bar whom they chose to favor, the English Crown now has not such absolute power. In England at the present day the bar *practically* chooses the judges. Constitutional methods in England, as every one knows, are largely matters of custom and precedent. Custom and precedent, there, have all, perhaps more than all, the force of our written constitutions. The British Crown cannot now appoint to judicial place any but the leading members of the bar; and leadership at the bar is acquired only by the exhibition of those qualities of mind and morals that recommend themselves to the admiration of every member of the bar. One class of lawyers in England employs another class; employment is naturally given to those only who are competent ; competency naturally wins its way to extensive practice and fame; and thus, while on the road upwards to place, the scrutiny of opponents and associates alike forms and establishes the character of the lawyer. Once at the head of his profession he becomes entitled, by a custom which has slowly grown to be now almost a part of the British constitution, to the next judicial place, and this right no government can deny him without danger. Thus, the British judges, though appointed by the government, are no longer tyrannous partisans (as they once were), but are substantially the choice of the British bar. The system of appointment by the executive never assumed this limitation in America; and, for this reason chiefly, the American system of appointment failed to give satisfaction to our democratic communities. The American people did not suffer, as the English people did, from judicial tyranny, but, with the jealous distrust of power that inheres in the nature of democracies, they saw that their judges were often appointed for other qualities than absolute merit and fitness, and they justly feared that the judicial power might some day be used to their serious detriment. They could not trust judges appointed for political considerations. They could not always have governors honest enough to be above political influences. Moreover, no American governor, with rare exceptions, had a sufficiently extensive acquaintanceship with members of the bar and their methods of practice to enable him, however honest his motive, to make the best choice. The people thought that they collectively were better capable of choosing their judges. So they took the power to themselves. But they have not been satisfied with the experiment. They have found themselves as frequently fooled and imposed upon as ever. The common sense of the matter would seem to be that it is essential to a proper system to provide some means of ascertaining scientifically what men are really worthy to be judges before proceeding either to appoint or elect judges.

It will, of course, be understood that the British bar does not exercise or claim any right to choose the judges. It simply selects, or evolves, a certain number of persons for its upper rank. By force of long usage, it has come to be obligatory on the Government to appoint one of this number only. The Government cannot now appoint obscure or untried men, though it has a choice among several known to be competent. The British judiciary, as a whole, for many years, has had the confidence and respect of the British people. Exceptions, no doubt, can be found, but truly it must be said, that taken all in all, it is the most satisfactory judiciary in the world.

I shall next speak of the system in vogue with us of nominating judges by partisan conventions ; but of this system I shall speak very briefly, because its defects must be already manifest. Traditional respect for the lofty nature of judicial functions has somewhat restrained these conventions from following their natural bent. For this reason we occasionally find conventions nominating candidates for judicial office without regard to political expediency or partisanship. But these cases are aberrations. Nominating conventions, of the sort I refer to, require only time to exhibit their true nature. Very soon judges are selected, or seem to be selected, for political reasons, or even for less worthy reasons. But, conceding to such bodies the utmost good faith, they are from their very nature totally incapable of testing or determining the fitness of lawyers for judicial place. They can neither possess the intimate acquaintance with the personality of the men, nor the accurate knowledge of the nature of the work to be done, that is essential to the exercise of an efficient choice.

It sometimes happens that "Bar Associations" recommend to nominating conventions or governors candidates for judicial place. As a rule, the persons so recommended are more suitable than those otherwise chosen, but this is by no means invariably the case, and there are several plain reasons why experiments in this direction have not succeeded as well as might be expected. The first reason is that owing to the inadequate salaries and short term of office offered by the State, only a comparatively small, and generally unsuccessful class of practitioners can be found willing to be candidates ; hence the choice afforded to the association is limited not to the most suitable but to the merely willing members of the bar. The most suitable men are absolutely excluded from choice. Another reason is that

the system of voting for candidates generally
in vogue within the " Bar Association " is not
calculated to obtain the unbiased judgment of
the individual members of the association. It
is a system of canvassing, and electioneering,
precisely similar to the system adopted by the
political conventions, except· that, generally
speaking, unworthy motives are not present /
in the minds of the friends of candidates. A
system of this sort is wholly unfit to determine
accurately what person stands highest in the
regard of the several members. Each member
is more or less biased or swayed by the advice
or entreaty of some other member or class of
members, and too often votes, not upon his
personal knowledge, nor for his first and personal choice, but upon the opinions of others,
and for the choice of others. Moreover, Bar
Associations, generally speaking, contain comparatively few members of the whole bar, and
thus not only is the choice of candidates offered to them meagre, and the method of voting illy calculated to stimulate the individual
independence and obtain the secret judgment
of the members, but, by reason of the comparatively small number of associates, the more

influential members have undue facilities for swaying the mass. I do not mean to be understood as intimating that, even under such conditions, Bar Associations ever consciously recommend any candidate from unworthy motives. I simply mean that they cannot select the best men at the bar ; that the stronger and more influential members have too great an influence to leave the choice of the Associations entirely free, and that they produce, in consequence, no result on the judicial system other than to put on the Bench weaker men than those who remain at the bar.

Finally, there is very little in the nature of the organizations tending to elevate their members above the rank and file of the profession, except what advantage may possibly be derived in manners from greater opportunities of social contact. These advantages, however, if they arise at all in any valuable degree, do not accrue to any persons outside the Association— often constituting the larger part of the profession. For Bar Associations are little more than social clubs. They have no powers derived from, or duties imposed by the State, and consequently share the fate of all men and

bodies who attempt to command without power
to enforce obedience. They are apt to be de-
spised by those whom they attempt to criticize,
and in turn to feel a sense of their own insig-
nificance, which is not encouraging to the
growth of civism. Being powerless to stem the
current of what they reprobate, the members
retain, as their first and chief thought, the interests of the clients from whom chiefly they
derive not only sustenance, but what little of
reputation can be obained in the practice of
the law under existing conditions. In proportion as the association is small in numbers and
its members eminent and able, so in proportion are they to be found in the employ of
those classes who have withdrawn so largely
the talent and capacity of the bar from the
service of the State. If those classes dominate
in the general affairs of the community, the
independence of the Bar Association, even in
respect to its utterances, is weakened in direct
proportion to the domination. This is spe-
cially noticeable in small communities of commercial activity, while it is not so observable
in larger places, or in small communities
where commercial activity is not great. Un-

doubtedly the New York Bar Association ob-
tains much of its comparatively greater independence of character from the very size of
the community, the consequent isolation of
the lawyers who compose it from each other,
and the isolation, and comparative powerless-
ness likewise, of individuals and interests that
might dominate in a smaller place. But everywhere the evils produced by our general judicial systems affect the *esprit de corps* and the
conduct of our Bar Associations, though sometimes in a less degree, always quite in the same
way, that they affect the public spirit and disinterestedness of the bar generally. To sum up,
the Associations have no power to utter a single legal command, nor can they be compelled
to exercise even the function of prosecution
when the greatest public need demands it; they
have no organization adequate to fulfil even
the slender public tasks they fitfully assume;
they can confer no reward for, nor even give
any protection to the exercise of honest independence. They have thus necessarily failed
to gratify all the hopes that prompted their
formation, but they have nevertheless done a
great work on the whole in keeping alive the

fires of high and suitable aspiration, and have demonstrated, by the trust which they have obtained in so many places, that the innate common sense of the people recognizes something of their nature as essential to our judicial systems, and is ready to confer upon the bar, properly organized, sufficient power to attain its noblest ends.

Let us ·recall our object. Our object is to place the stronger and more influential men upon the Bench ; to deprive them of the undue weight and power they now exercise for interests adverse to the interests of the general public ; to identify their interests and aspirations with the interests and aspirations of the entire people, and to elevate surely and permanently the character and capacity of the entire Bar.

I have intimated that the proper and most suitable persons for judicial place are such as should be selected or evolved for the purpose by a scientific system which will bring into action, if humanly possible, the freest, least biased, most disinterested and most intelligent choice *of each and every member of the*

whole bar. It seems to me that I need not
argue that such a method is the true republican method of obtaining judges for a republican community. We have constant evidence
that this is the opinion of the most intelligent.
of our fellow-citizens outside of the legal profession. When a judge goes wrong, or offends
public judgment, lawyers as a class are re-
proached, or called upon to take action. The
public assumes that the legal profession should
possess and exercise an influence in the selection of judges, and at least a disciplinary power over members of the bar. Common sense
dictates that the best persons to estimate ex-
cellence in any art, trade or calling are persons who follow that art, trade or calling.
The judgment of painters upon painting; of
musicians upon music; of architects upon ar-
chitecture ; of mechanicians upon mechanics,
was confessed by the populace in the days of
Plato to be the best sort of judgment. Our people are not afraid to concede to their lawyers
presumptive superiority in discerning their
most excellent members. Still, it is not to be
expected, nor would it be advisable, that the
people shall relegate to the lawyers the power

of appointing the judges without control or choice on the part of the body of the people. The utmost that is necessary or advisable is to concede to the lawyers the power of selecting a number of persons from whom the people can safely choose, and whose characters and attainments, after being certified to by the lawyers, may be scrutinized by the people at large.

When we reflect also that no government can exist without a judiciary, that this judiciary must necessarily be chosen exclusively from the lawyers, we perceive at once that the whole body of lawyers is in reality a part of the judicial system of the State. But when the State grants to a citizen a license to practice law, it confers upon him under our present system a powerful privilege, without demanding from him the exercise of any civic duty in his capacity as a factor of the judicial arm of the government. It is this duty, necessarily resulting from and existing in a license to practice law, that the people at large dimly perceive when they blame the body of lawyers for any fault in our judicial system. And as it is

essential to the proper exercise of those civic
duties attaching to the profession of the law
that the profession at large shall be given the
power necessary for the purpose, we easily perceive not only that the lawyers should designate those fit to be judges, but that the whole
body of the lawyers should be organized for
the purpose of making the choice and enforcing discipline.

Many more reasons might be given by me
in support of this fundamental idea, but I
deem it better for the sake of brevity to state
at once the outlines of the system of organization I propose, with the hope that the more reflection is given to it, the deeper will grow con-
viction that it has been in general accurately
conceived. Of course, I do not mean to assert
that improvements may not at once present
themselves to many minds in the details of the
system. Nor do I mean to say that in matter
of detail, if the system is ever put in practice,
experience may not demonstrate the advisability or necessity of some other changes.

III.

OUTLINES OF THE PROPOSED SYSTEM.

The general plan, underlying the system I propose, is that the bar shall, by the Constitution of the State, be included within the judicial system of the State, and the whole judicial system thus created shall be so organized that its functions shall serve: (A) to establish and maintain suitable qualifications for admission to its several ranks; (B) to establish and maintain suitable discipline within its several ranks; and (C) to naturally evolve a number of lawyers, proven to be fitted in character and attainments, for the judicial office, from whom the judges shall be chosen by the people.

To render this general plan comformable to our ideas of government, I suggest details that are subsidiary to, and limit or aid the general plan. The most essential of these details are so designed: (D) that the bar shall not be permitted to assume an un-democratic or un-

American form ; and (E) that its best members shall be willing to become judges when
chosen by the people. Other details, almost as
essential, are likewise applied, viz.: (F) that
while every citizen shall find wherever there is
a free American High School *adequate* means
of freely acquiring the necessary academic preparation for *entrance* upon the *study* of the law,
and no citizen shall be excluded from the bar
on account of fortuitous circumstances like race,
color, poverty or number of persons already at
the bar, nevertheless no person shall be able to
finally enter the bar without adequate knowledge of the law and appreciation of the nature
of the duties of a lawyer to himself, his clients
and the State; (G) that while the system of enforcing discipline at the bar shall be adequate
to maintain a high standard of professional
conduct, it shall not be so rigid as to destroy
individual force of character; (H) that while
the choice of candidates for the Bench shall be
limited to those persons whose character and
capacity are ascertained and certified by the
bar, and while adequate means shall be adopted
to secure the independence of the judiciary,
there shall also be such ready means of enforc-

ing proper judicial conduct that popular clamor against the judiciary shall become equally unnecessary and disgraceful.

I shall now state the outlines of such a system as I think sufficient for the accomplishment of the ends in view. Details shall be stated with special reference to conditions existing in the State of California, because I am more familiar at present with conditions in that State. But I must not be understood as attempting to employ, at any place in this article, language sufficiently exact for actual employment in the laws I suggest. My design is only to suggest outlines and purposes, even where I appear to enter into details. It will be found, however, that with alterations, or special forms of legislation, that will readily suggest themselves, the general system can be adapted to the needs of every State; and I shall consequently leave to the reader the task of altering and suiting the method to his own ideas of statutory forms and the exigencies of any particular state.

FIRST. The service of the State shall be made attractive as a career by suitable salaries, tenure of office during good behavior and retiring allowance. *This is a condition without which the*

*best class of lawyers cannot be obtained for the
Bench under any system,* as I have already endeavored to show.

Provisions for the retirement of incapacitated
judges and for the removal of unworthy judges
will be stated hereafter.

SECOND. The whole bar of the State shall be
divided into sections or chapters, and each
chapter shall be required to select, in the manner hereinafter stated, a Council of Juristic
Discipline, which shall be convertible as hereafter described, into a Court of Juristic Discipline. In general terms, the division of the
bar into sections or chapters shall be so ar-
ranged: (a) that the several members of each
chapter shall be residents, or have offices within the same territorial district, so as to enable
them to assemble when necessary, with as little
inconvenience as possible; (b) that the number
of members in each chapter shall be as nearly
equal as possible; (c) that each chapter shall
contain a sufficient number of lawyers to afford
ample choice in selecting members for the
Councils or Courts of Discipline. For example,
the State of California may be conveniently divided for this purpose into five territorial dis-

tricts, each containing about as many lawyers as now practice in the City of San Francisco, and each district, chapter, or section of the bar will be large enough to elect an efficient Council or Court of Juristic Discipline containing as many members as there are judges of the Superior Courts of Record within the district. (It will be obvious that in some States in which there are large cities, it may not be necessary or advisable to found the chapters of the bar on territorial limitations merely. If the numerical strength of the bar be sufficiently great in a thickly populated district, more than one chapter may be established within such a district, and no obligation imposed upon the members of any chapter to reside in any particular part of the district. In other words, in such cases the chapters may be established upon maximum and minimum limitations in point of numbers, and every lawyer in the district be associated by lot, or otherwise, with a particular chapter within the district. Details of this kind are not material.)

THIRD. Each section or chapter shall be required to assemble within its district, and elect from among those of its members who shall

have been practicing ten years and over, a
Council (convertible into a Court) of Juristic
Discipline. The number of persons constituting this Council of Discipline shall, in California, be about equal to the number of judges
of the Superior Court within the district. The
elections shall be by the Australian Ballot System, that is to say: the clerk of the Supreme
Court (who has custody of the roll of attorneys)
shall be required to print a suitable number of
ballots for each chapter, every ballot containing
in alphabetical order the names of every lawyer
of ten years' standing on the roll of the Court,
and having an office within the district relegated to the chapter. Every duly admitted
practitioner within the district (chapter) shall
be entitled to vote for the whole number of
members of the Council of Juristic Discipline,
and the persons receiving the highest number
of votes shall be declared elected, except as fol-
lows: not more than one member of any co-
partnership of lawyers shall ever, at the same
time, be eligible to a seat in the Council ; and
while the name of every lawyer of over ten
years' standing must appear on the ballot,
whether he be in co-partnership or not, if at an

election more than one member of a co-partnership shall appear to be chosen, only the member
of the co-partnership who shall receive the
highest number of votes, as between all the co-
partners, shall be deemed elected, and the votes
cast for the other members of the co-partnership shall be deemed to have been cast for
him. (N. B.—The provision against allowing
more than one member of a co-partnership to
belong to the council at the same time should
be made permanent, to prevent the undue as-
cendency of great firms ; but the method of
limiting the choice to one member of a firm is
intended only for the first elections. When
organized, the chapters may be trusted to
devise, if necessary, a better method within
the lines of the Australian system.) The first
meetings of these several chapters shall be
presided over by one of the Justices of the
Supreme Court appointed for the purpose by
the Governor ; the president so appointed to
have charge of the ballots, and be entrusted
with the duty of conducting the election.
This duty will, of course, include the duty of
seeing that no one but regularly admitted practitioners having offices within the district be

allowed to vote ; that an oath be administered
to each practitioner that he shall, without bias
or any other motive than the public good,
vote for those persons only as members of the
Council of Discipline who, in his private opinion, are by character and attainments most
worthy to perform the duties assigned to them
as members of the Council of Discipline and
, thereafter to become judges. Provision shall
be made empowering the president of these
initial meetings to compel by fine, or by suspension from practice, the attendance and vote
of each and every member of the bar within
the district.   The method of calling the meetings is non-essential ; but I deem requirements
that the voting shall be by ballot ; that none
but lawyers of ten years' standing shall be
eligible to be members of the Council of Discipline ; and that all the members of the chapter shall be required to vote, unless, of course,
sick or absent from the State, essential for the
proper working of the system.

FOURTH.   Whenever the term of office of
any of the present judges of the Superior Court
within any district is about to expire, the
name of such judge with the names of all the

members of the Council of Juristic Discipline
of the district shall be printed on the State
ballot as candidates, from among whom the
people at large may choose a new judge; and
no other person shall be eligible for the office.
Of course, when a vacancy occurs on the
Superior Bench by reason of the death, voluntary retirement, or removal from office of any
of the present incumbents, only the names of
the members of the Council of Juristic Discipline of the district shall be printed on the
State ballot as candidates. And when a member of the Council of Juristic Discipline is
elected judge, or dies, or is removed from the
council for any cause, the vacancy in the council shall be immediately filled by the chapter
at an election to be conducted on the Australian ballot system, as provided in paragraph 3.

As seen up to this point, the proposed system presents at least these points of advantage:
(a) the Bench is made attractive to the ablest
class of lawyers; (b) no one but a lawyer of at
least ten years' standing, or a judge already
tested, can be elected to the Superior Bench.
There is, moreover, little likelihood that com-

binations will be formed to promote unworthy
men to the Bench. All the general arguments
in favor of the Australian ballot system apply
in support of the belief that the choice made
by the chapters will be as good as is humanly
possible under any democratic form of government so far as hitherto developed. Professional jealousy will give added caution to each
lawyer in casting his vote, for every man will
desire to select only such men as will give him
an equal chance with every one of his brethren
in a trial for breach of discipline. And no set
of lawyers sufficiently numerous to elect a
single member of the Disciplinary Council can
expect to be always employed on the same side
in every litigation in the ordinary Courts.
They must anticipate that at some time in their
professional career they may find themselves
opponents of each other. Hence, every lawyer's interest is to secure not only impartial
members of the Councils of Discipline, but
members who are likely to be unbiased judges.
Moreover, the people at large have the ultimate
scrutiny of all the candidates for the Bench
and the ultimate selection of the judge.

I propose, however, to add another powerful

incentive to a careful choice by the bar. I propose to confer upon those Councils of Juristic Discipline such weighty powers over each and every member of the profession as will not, from motives of self-preservation, be entrusted by the bar to any but its best men.

FIFTH. Every Council of Juristic Discipline shall be vested with power (1st) to issue licenses to practice law; (2nd) to hear and determine, as a Court, all charges of unprofessional conduct brought against members of the chapter; (3rd) to inflict disciplinary punishment for infractions of professional ethics; and (4th) to exercise such other powers as may be conferred on it by the chapter, or by general convention of the bar, as hereafter provided. When sitting as a Court for the trial of a member of the bar, I propose that the Council shall be organized and conduct its proceedings somewhat after the manner of courts-martial; that is to say, that the number of members of the Council necessary to constitute a Court of Juristic Discipline shall be fixed; that the accused and the accuser shall have suitable rights of challenging the members of the Court for bias; that the votes of

the Court on the question submitted to it shall
be kept secret; that the Court shall have power
to issue subpœnas, punish for contempt, and so
forth. Of course, to guard against arbitrary
conduct there may be power reserved in the
Supreme Court to restrain excess of jurisdiction
by *certiorari*, etc. But details of all these matters may be relegated to the care of the General
Council of the bar hereafter described.

As it is manifest that general provisions
should be made of uniform application throughout the State for the qualifications of persons
applying for admission to the bar; for the officers necessary to properly conduct the business
of the chapters; for the organization of the
councils into Courts of Juristic Discipline, and
for procedure on trials for infraction of professional ethics; and as it may be advisable, in the
opinion of the bar, to confer other powers or
duties of a disciplinary nature on these councils, I propose an Assembly of all the Councils
of the several chapters to be held at some particular place in the State within a suitable
period after the first election of the councils.

SIXTH. All of the Councils of Discipline

elected by the various chapters of the bar shall be required to meet as one body within a certain period after their election at some place within the State, and there enact a Code of Juristic Discipline:

(A) Providing the course of study to be pursued by persons studying law outside of law schools; the times and places for the periodic examinations of students, as hereafter required; the method of registering law students, and the results of their periodic examinations on the books of the several chapters; and the ultimate qualifications for admission to the bar. (Certain other matters pertaining to legal education shall be rigidly provided for by law, as hereafter stated, without power in the General Council of the bar to interfere therewith.)

(B) Defining the general duties of a lawyer; his duty toward his client; his duty toward his brother lawyers; his duty toward the judges; and his duty toward the State.

(C) Providing, so far as may appear necessary, for a uniform constitution for the several chapters : that is to say, prescribing the necessary administrative officers with common powers and duties ; common methods and times for calling meetings of the members of the chapters; and regulating all other matters in which it may appear advisable to preserve uniformity in the business methods of the several chapters, but leaving to each chapter sufficient freedom to enact special by-laws suitable to its local (or otherwise peculiar) conditions.

(D) Prescribing the penalties to be inflicted by Courts of Juristic Discipline for unprofessional conduct on the part of members of the bar.

(E) Regulating the method of organizing the councils into Courts of Juristic Discipline for the trial of members of the bar, and the procedure on such trials.

(F) Regulating the method of organizing the councils into Courts of Juristic Discipline for preliminary inquiries into charges affecting the conduct of judges, as hereinafter provided, and the procedure on such inquiries.

(G) Regulating the method of organizing the councils into Courts of Inquiry concerning the retirement of incapacitated judges, as hereinafter provided, and the procedure on such inquiries.

The project of empowering this representa-

tive body of lawyers to provide for certain
details of legal education will probably meet
with neither serious objection nor approval
from the general reader. Nor will there be
any serious objection to empowering this body
to regulate the methods of organizing the various disciplinary courts spoken of, or the course
of procedure at trials before those courts, provided the advisability of having the courts as
part of the judicial system of the State sufficiently appears. When the further details of
the reform I propose are read, proper reflection
can be given by the reader to all these matters.

It will doubtless appear, however, to some
minds, trivial to require an elaborate statement
of ethical rights and duties in the practice of
their profession, and a table of penalties for
unprofessional conduct, to proceed from this
body. To other minds, the objection will occur that the Code of Civil Procedure of this
State has already announced, with all the force
of legislative enactment, the duties of attorneys
and counselors, and no greater force would
attach to a declaration of those duties proceeding from a representative body of lawyers than
now attaches to the section of the Code of Pro-

cedure. Since these objections cannot suitably
be considered elsewhere in this essay, a few
words on these subjects may be pardoned here.

That we must have some code or standard of
ethics for the government of attorneys and
counselors at law in the practice of their profession cannot be gainsaid so long as there re-
mains on the Statute-book such a section as
Section 282 of the Code of Civil Procedure.
For the benefit of lay readers of this essay, I
reproduce here that section :

" Section 282.   It is the duty of an attorney
" and counselor :

" 1.   To support the Constitution and laws
" of the United States and of this State ;

" 2.   To maintain the respect due to courts
" and judicial officers ;

" 3.   To counsel or maintain such actions,
" proceedings, or defenses only as appear to
" him legal or just, except the defense of a per-
" son charged with a public offense ;

" 4.   To employ for the purpose of maintain-
" ing the causes confided to him such means
" only as are consistent with truth, and never
" seek to mislead a judge, or any judicial offi-
" cer by an artifice, or false statement of fact
" or law ;

" 5. , To maintain inviolate the confidence,
" and at every peril to himself, to preserve the
" secrets of his client ;

" 6. To abstain from all offensive personal-
" ity, and to advance no fact prejudicial to the
" honor or reputation of a party or witness,
" unless required by the justice of the cause
" with which he is charged ;

" 7. Not to encourage the commencement
" or continuance of an action or proceeding
" from any corrupt motive of passion or in-
" terest ;

" 8. Never to reject, for any consideration
" personal to himself, the cause of the defense-
" less or the oppressed."

If this section is carefully analyzed it will be
seen that the Legislature imposes upon attorneys and counselors many duties which, though
absolutely essential to the proper and honest
discharge of their functions, are habitually disregarded. This is principally because the conditions surrounding the practice of the law
under our judicial system are such that the duty
to the client almost obliterates every other sense
of duty. The client's interests overween the
State's interests, because the client possesses

and employs adequate means both of rewarding successful and punishing unsuccessful methods. The State, on the other hand, neither offers suitable rewards for observance of the duties of lawyers toward it, nor provides tribunals suitable to examine cases of alleged infraction and punish delinquencies. The fact is undoubted that most of the provisions of Section 282 of the Code of Civil Procedure are habitually disregarded by otherwise honorable lawyers, because most of the duties seem impossible to be strictly observed, under existing conditions, and hence are not binding on professional consciences. The only duty imposed by the State that is rarely disregarded, and when disregarded ever meets with adequate punishment, is the duty to the client. For while it is true that the Supreme Court possesses the power of punishing lawyers for all breaches of professional ethics, it commonly moves against and punishes only cases of gross swindling or deception. I think I have never heard of a charge being made against a lawyer for failing to maintain the respect due to Courts and judicial officers, though I have often heard lawyers malign judges; nor have I heard of a charge of counseling an il-

legal or unjust action; or indulging in offensive
personality; or of advancing unnecessarily facts
prejudicial to the honor of a witness; or of encouraging an action from a corrupt motive of
passion or interest; yet, though I do not intend
unnecessarily to disparage my profession, if all
the infractions of those duties that occur daily
were brought to the attention of the Court for
adjudication, it is not unlikely that the Court
would have little time to spare for any work on
the congested mass of litigation now before it.

The Supreme Court is thus, obviously, not a
tribunal adequate to preserve such discipline as
the Legislature has enacted for the bar.   I propose to confer upon the bar itself the power to
discipline its members.   The English bar does
this effectively through the Benchers of its
Inns of Court.   The French bar has always
been effectively organized for its own government, and through all the revolutions and
changes of society in France has maintained a
very high standard of professional honor.   It
has always had similar bodies to the Councils
of Discipline which I propose.   Long ago these
bodies formulated a thoroughly practical and
elevating code of professional ethics (which is

little more than an elaboration of the duties of attorneys and counselors prescribed by our code) and provided different kinds of disciplinary punishment, viz.: "the Warning," " the Private Reprimand," " the Public Reprimand," " Temporary Suspension from Practice," "Total Expulsion from the Profession." There is very little in the French code of professional ethics which is unsuited to our methods, and which might not be adopted by us with thoroughly good results. But even if we cannot expect our bar to be so rigid in its discipline, we can obtain from it, at least, a statement of some simple duties which it is willing to acknowledge. The voluntary statement of a duty is, to any set of men that ventures to state it, a substantial stimulus to the performance of the duty; and if there be a tribunal charged with the power of enforcing the performance of that duty, composed of the best men who have assisted in enunciating the duty, we shall have a still greater stimulus to its general performance. Supposing that the tone of our bar is now so low that it will only enunciate the simplest duties, still, from the exercise of simple duties a knowledge and appreciation of the value of more refined duties will in time arise. If it be not true that there is a subtler and more powerful compulsion to perform a duty we have voluntarily assumed, and to obey tribunals we have ourselves constituted, than there is to perform duties and obey tribunals forcibly imposed upon us by others, then there is no ground for all our hope in self-government. Self-government according to function is surely the complement of the ideas of national and local self-government.

For these reasons, and others which space prevents me from elaborating, I propose to confer upon the bar power to discipline itself according to a code, and through officers of its own choice; and I propose to recruit our Bench from the most worthy members of a self-respecting bar. This will superadd to our system the best feature of the modern English bar, viz.: its influence on the choice of judges, and the best feature of the French bar, viz.: its system of maintaining the integrity of its members. The English system evolves to the front rank the best and most honorable lawyers for the purpose of providing judges ; the French system, while it does not provide judges (for the French judges are not selected

from the bar, but are a special profession), still
maintains admirably the integrity of its advo-
cates.   Granting the superior American talent for self-government, the American system
should be better than either.

SEVENTH.   The judges of the Supreme Court
(Court of Appeals) shall be chosen by, and
from among, the judges of the Superior Court
(highest Court of original jurisdiction).   Whenever a judge of the Supreme Court is to be
elected, the name of the out-going judge (if
there be one) shall be printed on a State ballot
with the names of all the judges of the Superior Courts, in alphabetical order.   This ballot
shall be furnished in sufficient numbers to a
general convocation of the judges of the Superior Courts, assembled for the purpose of elect-
ing a person to fill the vacancy on the Supreme
Bench.   Each Superior Judge shall be entitled
to two votes, one to be termed "first choice,"
and the other "second choice."   The person
receiving the highest number of votes to be
declared elected.

The classical origin of this method of voting will be readily perceived.   Each judge

may vote for himself for first choice, while all
may unite on a Solon for second choice. Solon
would be elected.

It is best for many reasons that the judges of
the high courts of original jurisdiction shall
select the judges of the Supreme Appellate
Courts. It often happens now that the Appellate Courts contain some judges of marked infe-
riority to some of the judges of the lower courts.
This is one great cause of uncertainty in the
law, and plainly is not conducive to respect for
the accuracy of ultimate judicial conclusions.
If the members of the appellate tribunal are
chosen by a method which implies an ac-
knowledgment of their peculiar adaptability
to the function — and that implied acknowl-
edgment is, moreover, made by the judicial
officers whose supposed errors are to be examined—the judgments of such a tribunal must of
necessity command the greatest weight. The
most logical method of selecting the members
of appellate tribunals, then, is by free vote of
the judges over whom they are to sit. But, if a
more " popular " system of election be pre-
ferred, a similar result might be reached (in a
lesser degree) by a law providing that no one

but a judge of the highest court of original jurisdiction shall be eligible for a seat in the Court of Appeals, and requiring that the names of all the judges of the lower court be printed on a State ballot, for choice by the body of the people. This latter method might, however, be a temptation to some judges to court "popularity," or at least attach to those elected the suspicion of having courted "popularity," and, therefore, I much prefer the idea of having the judges of the lower courts select their superior officers. If militia men may select company officers, and those officers again may select field officers, it is not plain to me why a similar method may not be followed in the judicial service of the State.

I now proceed to the next general propositions — which relate to preparation for and admission to the Bar :

EIGHTH. No Court shall possess power to admit persons to the practice of the law, but instead, every Council of Juristic Discipline throughout the State shall appoint an Examiner of law students ; all the Examiners shall act together as a board, and be required to at-

tend, once in each year, within every district,
for the purpose of examining all such persons
as shall desire to enter upon and those who
may be already pursuing the study of the law
with the intention of becoming law practitioners. It shall be the duty of the Board of
Examiners to strictly examine every person
applying to be enrolled as a student at law in
respect to his general educational qualifications
and moral character. Every person applying
to be enrolled as a law student, and who shall
pass such an examination as is required for
graduation at a free high school of the State,
or for admission to a State university, shall be
enrolled in the books of the chapter of the bar
within whose district he intends to pursue his
studies, and shall thereafter be examined every
year, by the Board of Legal Education, in respect to his advancement in the course of
study prescribed by the General Council of the
bar, and a suitable record kept of his progress,
unless he shall give proof that he is in regular
attendance at some law school requiring an
adequate course of study. No person pursuing
his law studies outside of a law school shall
be admitted to practice law until he shall have

pursued a course of five years' study and shall
have successfully passed all the annual examinations. Every person, whether attending a
law school or not, who shall enter upon the
study of the law with the intention of becoming a practitioner, shall first be enrolled as a
law student, with a statement of the method
by which he intends to pursue his studies, on
the books of the local Council of Juristic Discipline, and shall be subject to such discipline
as the council may enact. But no fees shall
ever be required for enrollment, examination
or admission to the bar, and no person shall
ever be refused admission as a student, or as
an attorney or counselor, on account of age,
color, physical infirmity or number of persons
already enrolled as students, attorneys or counselors. Every student, before final admission
as attorney or counselor (whether he may
have studied within or without a law school),
shall be finally examined as to his qualifications by the Board of Legal Education, who, if
he shall satisfactorily acquit himself, must re-
port the fact to the local Council of Juristic
Discipline, and the council shall be required
thereupon (unless he has been disciplined for

cause) to issue to him a license to practice law
in all the Courts of the State. Thereupon, he
shall be enrolled as a member of whatever
chapter of the bar may exercise its functions
within the district selected by him for com-
mencing practice.

The subject of legal education is a very large
one, and I shall touch only upon such aspects of
it as will serve to elucidate some of the ideas
contained in the last preceding provisions. It
is a singular fact that, though the legal profession has never been jealous of the admission
of new members, there yet grew up in the
minds of the people of the United States, about
the " Forties," an idea that the profession was
exclusive and aristocratic. As a result, an eminent member of the New York bar infected
the popular mind many years ago with the
vicious notion that every one who chose to apply should be permitted to practice law, because (he argued) only those who were competent could succeed. While this notion is
supported by the undoubted facts that a lawyer's work must always run the gauntlet of
criticism and opposition, and that entirely incompetent men cannot make great successes,

more important facts, that in time demonstrated the falsity of the theory, were over-
looked for many years. The law is not a profession which can be followed by illiterate, incompetent, or dishonest men, without inflicting
the gravest injuries not only upon clients, but
also upon the entire body politic. While a
man is demonstrating his special unfitness to
be a lawyer (and perhaps making money in
the process), he may ruin many a client, or in-
troduce many a scandalous practice irretrieva-
bly injurious to the reputation of legal methods
in general. They found this out in New York
after an interval of about twenty-five years,
and recognized, almost too late, what would
seem to be apparent at first sight, viz.: that the
State owes the duty to itself and to its citizens
that its license to practice law shall import
that the individual to whom it is issued has
given some evidence of adequate attainments.
So the State of New York has, within the past
ten years, begun to make some stringent requirements for admission to practice.

California (following the earliest crudities)
has, in order to provide its citizens with *competent* lawyers, made a futile enactment that

" every applicant for admission as attorney
" and counselor must produce satisfactory tes-
" timonials of good moral character, and un-
" dergo *a strict examination in open court* " (! ! !)
" as to his qualifications by the justices of the
" Supreme Court," etc., and so disposes of the
whole matter. With the best intentions in the
world, our overworked judges cannot adequate-
ly perform all that they know to be necessary
and that is here impliedly required of them.
Consequently, there are persons at the bar who
must have obtained their " satisfactory testimonials of good moral character " in a former
state of existence, and who, if they ever under-
went a " *strict* examination " in open court as
to their professional qualifications, were on that
lucky day gifted by Providence with a miracu-
lous intellect " for the occasion only." This
must be apparent to many judges before whom
some of the practioners they created now appear. So I conclude that a single examination
of " *testimonials* of good moral character," and
" qualifications in the law," however much the
Legislature may require it to be *strict*, cannot
give such assurance of capacity for the practice
of the law as a probationary period of five

years, passed under watchful eyes, with power
to discipline for unbecoming conduct, and with
periodical examinations into the diligence, capacity and advancement of the student. If a
single *strict* "examination in open court" is
advisable for the State's purposes, surely a
yearly examination for five years will be more
advantageous. True, some students may have
greater minds than others and be prepared
sooner for the work of life ; but such lucky
men can afford to wait, for they will bring
with them to the bar superior reputations.

Moreover, the time of the Courts should be
devoted to other work than this of examining
students—highly important though the work is.
I propose, in view of its importance and the
labor it involves, to have it performed in another and better way. And. while I provide
that no one who can attend and profit by the
free public schools shall find the profession of
the law closed to him for any undemocratic
reason, I provide also that the State shall be as-
sured that its license to practice law cannot be
obtained by any one unfit to hold it.

NINTH. The State shall pay reasonable salaries to the examiners to be appointed under this

system; it shall also pay traveling expenses and *per diem* allowances to the members of the General Council of Juristic Discipline, while in session, equal in amount to the allowances made to members of the Legislature; it shall also pay like *per diem* allowances to the members of every Court of Juristic Discipline for every day engaged in the actual hearing of trials.

If I am right in hoping that the general system which I propose will in time elevate the character of the bench and bar, and will in time inspire public confidence in the administration of justice, surely no money can be better expended by the State. Leaving out of view the inestimable value of an increased self-respect as Americans, the financial saving that will be effected by a well ordered judicial system is incalculable. There ought to be no hesitancy to provide suitable salaries for such important functionaries as persons charged with the duty of training and examining American youth for admission to the American bar. And as to the *per diem* allowances suggested for members of the Disciplinary Courts while in actual session, it ought to be sufficient to point out that such allowances will rarely be adequate "compensa-

tion" to the persons likely to be members of
such Courts for the time withdrawn from their
regular practice for the performance of the
duties imposed on them; and, consequently
(following the principle on which we pay members of our Legislature), the payments suggested are mainly intended to emphasize the duties
imposed, and their effect to relieve somewhat
the burden of performance is a mere incident.

TENTH. All licenses to practice law at present held, and all licenses hereafter granted, shall
be held and granted upon condition that the
holder shall accept the office, and diligently fulfil
all the duties of member of any and every Council or Court of Juristic Discipline to which he
may be elected.. If any person shall decline to
accept the office of member of a Council of Discipline, except for physical incapacity to perform
its duties, or if any person shall decline to act
as a member of a Court of Discipline, except for
actual bias or interest in the result of a trial,
such person shall *ipso facto* cease to be a member of the bar. If a member of a Council of
Discipline shall desire not to accept the office ·
of judge, he must announce his unwillingness in

writing to the chapter of the bar to which he
belongs, within a stated period (say not less than
three months) before the time appointed by
law for the next election of judges at which his
name would otherwise appear as one of the
chosen candidates. Upon such announcement
the member declining to become a candidate for
judge shall *ipso facto* cease to be a member of
the Council of Discipline, and forever after be
ineligible to be a member of any Council or
Court of Juristic Discipline, and an election
shall forthwith be held by the chapter of the
bar to which he belongs to fill his place in the
council. He shall not, however, be restricted in
the practice of his profession or otherwise disciplined for his refusal to become a judge.

If the State should offer its judges salaries
so large that no practice at the bar, however
lucrative, would afford an equal income, there
would be no injustice in providing that if a
lawyer, having physical capacity to perform
the duties, shall refuse to accept the office of
member of a Council of Juristic Discipline, or
that of judge when elected thereto, he shall
ipso facto cease to have the right to practice
law. But salaries as large as the largest re-

wards of private practice are hardly to be expected from the State. Liberal salaries and
tenure of office during good behavior, with
retiring allowances to faithful judges, are absolutely essential to, and if they are granted will
insure the successful working of the reform I
propose ; but salaries, tenure of office and retiring allowances may be liberal and sufficient,
and yet there may sometimes arise such a case
as that of a member of the bar receiving a
larger income from his profession than the salary attached to the office of judge, but having
a large family to maintain, and requiring all
his professional income for the maintenance of
his family. The injustice of forcing a man,
under such circumstances, to surrender his
necessary means of support would operate
strongly, in many minds, against the radical
measure of expelling him from the bar for refusal to become judge. But, on the other
hand, some minds may apprehend that since
it is almost certain that the most successful
lawyers will be chosen for the members of the
Councils of Juristic Discipline, and since no one
but a member of one of those councils is eligible to be a judge, there is danger that combi-

nations may be formed among some members
of the councils to decline to accept the office of
judge, and thus, by limiting the number of candidates to be presented to the people, such
combinations might practically appoint to the
Bench persons of their own selection. It might
be apprehended, moreover, that if, after having so managed to select a judge, the members
of the council unwilling to be judges remain in
the council, they will possess a most unwhole-
some influence, if not practical control over
the Bar and Bench; for, so long as the combination continued, only the newly elected members
of the council would be presented as candidates for the office of judge, and the linger-
ing members of the council would practically
be governors of the bar and nominators of
the judges. Now, while I regard it equally unlikely that any lawyer shall refuse to go on the
Bench, or that there will arise any such combinations, *if the State will offer reasonably liberal salaries, tenure of office and retiring allowances, and put into operation the other measures
of reform I have and shall indicate*, still, to
relieve the apprehensions that arise in so
many minds, that there is lurking danger in

every scheme of reform, I have endeavored to provide here, as everywhere throughout the system, a practical safe-guard against abuse. Hence, I provide in this tenth step of reform that every lawyer, without exception, *must* serve on the Councils and Courts of Juristic Discipline, if elected thereto, and thus be offered an opportunity to go on the Bench if chosen by the people ; nevertheless, if any person, eligible to the Bench, shall prefer the rewards of private practice, he must take his place in the rank and file of his profession, to pursue his financial aims subject to the supervision of better or less necessitous men.

I advance now to some general propositions for the discipline of the Bench:

ELEVENTH. The Governor, or any District Council of Discipline, shall have power to convene a General Court of Juristic Discipline for the purpose of hearing any accusations that may be brought against a judge for conduct unbecoming the judicial office. The General Court of Juristic Discipline assembled for this purpose shall consist (if deemed advisable) of a larger number of members than a Court of

Juristic Discipline for the trial of a member of the bar. And, in order that local prejudice or passion shall not sway the Court, its members shall be chosen from all the Councils of Juristic Discipline throughout the State by lot, with challenges allowed for bias, etc., as juries are selected from a large panel. The inquiry of the General Court of Juristic Discipline shall merely be : Is there reasonable ground to believe that conduct unbecoming a judicial officer has been committed by the accused ; and the judgment shall extend only to a suspension of the accused judge until such time as he may be tried by the ordinary High Court of Impeachment of the State. The General Court of Juristic Discipline shall be granted all necessary powers to conduct its proceedings and may appoint prosecutors before the Court of Impeachment, if deemed necessary.

TWELFTH. The Governor, or any District Council of Discipline, shall have power to convene a General Court of Juristic Discipline to act as a retiring board, in case it shall appear that any judge has become physically or mentally incapable of performing the duties of his office, and such Court so assembled shall have power to retire the judge for cause shown.

THIRTEENTH. Every chapter of the bar shall designate a place for the preservation of its records, and a place for holding its meetings, and for the meetings of the Council of Discipline elected by it. At the request of any chapter of the bar, the Board of Supervisors (or other suitable county officials) shall be required to provide suitable rooms and furniture for keeping the records of the chapter, and for the meetings of the chapter and of its Council of Discipline.

FOURTEENTH. Whenever any member of a Council of Discipline shall, in any manner, become aware that any charge has been made against any judge or member of the bar, of official or professional misconduct, or inefficiency, or of conduct which might have a tendency to impair respect for the administration of the law, it shall be the duty of such member of the Council of Discipline, within twenty-four hours after he shall have received such information, to serve notice in writing, through the mails, on each and every other member of the council to assemble at a specified time, which shall be not less than than four days thereafter, at the meeting place designated by the chapter of the bar for the transaction of its business, then and there to consider what may be necessary to be done in respect to such charge. The failure of ·the member of the council becoming aware of such charge to issue and mail the notices above required within twenty-four hours after he becomes aware of the charge, or the failure of any member of the council to attend when notified, shall *ipso facto* cause his suspension from practice, and he shall not be restored to the right to practice, unless he shall by affidavit, filed in the records of the chapter, make oath that such failure was in no wise deliberate, and state the true cause of such failure.

FIFTEENTH. The members of the Council so assembled shall forthwith inquire into the nature of the charges, and shall be vested with the necessary powers for pursuing the inquiry, and shall, if it appear to be proper and necessary, be empowered to issue a warrant for the assembling of a suitable Court of Juristic Discipline or Court of Inquiry as before provided.

The object of the two last provisions is to enable the public to force the bar to take cogni-
zance of and act upon scandals affecting the
administration of justice. Thus the humblest
citizen may set in motion the whole machinery
of the System of Discipline against the merest
" shyster," or the highest judge.

I observe, once more, that the foundation of
judicial reform is better salaries, tenure of
office during good behavior, suitable provision
for a faithful public servant on retirement, and
a scientific method of evolving the best men for
the Bench. Unless the people are willing to
concede all this not much can be done; once
granted, every safe-guard that can be devised
to promote discipline and prevent the growth
of a bureaucratic or exclusive spirit should be
welcomed. Valuable additions to or alterations
in the details of the system I propose, no doubt
can be suggested, but, in the main, I submit
that it is a practical method of creating an organized bench and bar, which, while in no sense
exclusive or bureaucratic in its spirit, but having its foundation on the American ideas of free

education and self-government, will nevertheless, by the very nature of the organization, of
necessity be true to the present needs of the
country and the perpetuation of democratic
government.

www.ingramcontent.com/pod-product-compliance
Lightning Source LLC
Chambersburg PA
CBHW031444270326
41930CB00007B/865